D1449393

Grandma Tolzmann's Christmas Cookies

cookies and recipes by
Irene Bernice Tolzmann

drawings by
Nathan Arlyn Tolzmann

ISBN 978-1-312-76178-0

In memory of Grandma Tolzmann
1916-1998

FOREWORD

When the cookie box from Grandma arrived before
Christmas in 1996 I decided to draw the cookies before
I ate them. I set up a desk lamp at the kitchen table and
drew one specimen of each variety. I called her and
asked her to bring along her recipes when she came to
visit. After Grandpa's death in 1982 it became an annual
tradition that she would come after Christmas and stay
with us for a bit of the winter. When she arrived we sat
at my parents' kitchen table and went over the recipes.
We double-checked all the ingredients and made sure
the instructions were clear. I drew a picture of Grandma
sitting in a chair in the family room. That's the drawing
on the cover of this book. When all the parts were
completed I photocopied the pages and hand-assembled
the pamphlets. It was a simple little book that Grandma
gave away many, many copies of. She would call me
when she needed a new batch. I'd copy and hand-
assemble more and send them to her. I was really glad
that we had made this thing together, especially because
she would only be around for one more Christmas. She
died on January 8, 1998.

I missed Grandma very much during 1998 and as Christmas approached my mom and I realized that we would also be missing the annual arrival of Grandma's cookie box. We opened *Grandma Tolzmann's Christmas Cookies* and started baking. We made boxes to send to other family members who would also be missing Grandma. Soon after sending out the boxes we received a box in the mail from my brother and his wife. It was a box of cookies that they had baked from Grandma's recipes.

Make these cookies and share them with your loved ones. Think of your grandma. I think of mine.

Nathan Tolzmann
2015

INTRODUCTION

In a world where Christmas traditions struggle to survive the advances of Christmas commercialism I am so glad for the traditions we do have. If we accept the traditions television has created for us, Macy's Thanksgiving Day parade is the official beginning of the Holiday season. Or maybe the Christmas season begins the next day with a country-wide migration to our local shopping malls. Well, there are those of us with more personal ideas about when Christmas begins. The arrival of Grandma's Christmas cookies has always been a more appropriate inaugural symbol of the season for me.

Grandma has been making cookies ever since she was able to lend Mom Carlson (my great-grandma) a hand, but the origin of her cookie boxes goes back to the Christmas of 1954. Grandpa, Grandma, Aunt Char, Uncle Brian, and my dad piled in the car and headed to California. They'd be spending the holidays with Grandma's sisters Minnie and Lil and their families. In the days before their departure Grandma had been busy baking so that on her arrival in California she was able to hand deliver a gift of homemade goodies.

Over the years Grandma continued to fix her care packages for friends and family. As her children grew up and moved away she found it necessary to start the preparations early so that she could send the packages on their way by the first weekend in December. The baking begins by the last week in October with cookies kept fresh in the freezer until all are ready to be shipped. She packs the boxes so carefully and with so much love that very few cookies ever seem to arrive broken. It would be hard to find a more reliable Christmas miracle.

Grandma sums up her reasons for sending out the boxes by saying, "I guess it's a part of my love going out to those people. It's not just going to the store to buy something."

Nathan Tolzmann
1996

CONTENTS

For family
its traditions
and the remembrance of both
throughout the year

CHOCOLATE PEANUT BUTTER DREAMS

1 1/2 C. packed brown sugar
1 C. creamy peanut butter
3/4 C. margarine
1/3 C. water
1 egg
1 t. vanilla
3 C. quick oats
1 1/2 C. flour
1/2 t. baking soda
1 1/2 C. chocolate chips
4 t. vegetable shortening
1/3 C. chopped peanuts

Heat oven to 350°. Beat together sugar, peanut butter and margarine until light and fluffy. Blend in water, egg, and vanilla. Add combined dry ingredients. Mix well. Shape into 1" balls. Place on ungreased cookie sheet. Flatten to 1/4" thickness with bottom of juice glass or a cookie stamp dipped in sugar. Bake 8-10 min. until edges are golden brown. Remove to wire rack. Cool completely. Over low heat melt chocolate and shortening. Stir until smooth. Top each cookie with 1/2 t. chocolate and sprinkle with chopped nuts. Chill until set. Store in airtight container. Makes 6 doz.

SCANDINAVIAN SLICED COOKIES

1 C. shortening
1 C. sugar
1 C. brown sugar
   3 eggs
 1 t. vanilla
 2 t. baking powder
    pinch of salt
4 C. flour
1 C. chopped nuts

Cream together the shortening with the sugar and brown sugar. Add eggs, vanilla, baking powder, salt, and flour. Lastly add the nuts. Mix and make into rolls. Place in a cool place over night. In morning slice and bake at 350° for 10-12 min. or until golden brown.

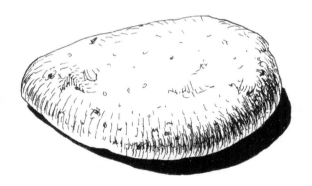

KRUMKAKER

1 C. sugar
1/2 C. butter
1/2 t. nutmeg
3 eggs
1 1/2 C. flour
1/2 C. whipping cream

Beat eggs until light. Add sugar, melted butter, cream, flour, and nutmeg. Bake on Krumkaker iron. Roll on cone or wooden handle immediately.

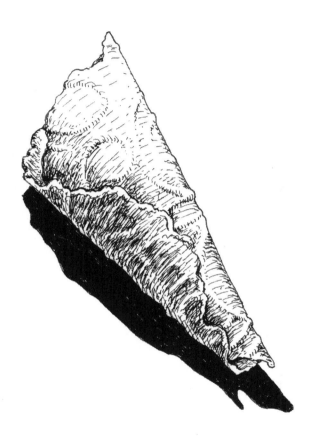

SAN BAKKELS

1 C. butter
1 C. sugar
1 egg
1/2 t. almond flavoring
3 C. flour

Cream butter and sugar. Add egg and stir well. Add flavoring. Add flour slowly. Stir well after each addition. Press into san bakkel tins with fingers. Bake at 300° for 10 min. or until golden brown. Remove from tins when cool enough to handle.

RUSSIAN TEA CAKES

    1 C. butter or margarine
  1/2 C. sifted confectioners' sugar
    1 t. vanilla
2 1/4 C. flour
  1/2 t. salt
  3/4 C. finely chopped nuts

Mix butter, sugar, and vanilla thoroughly.
Measure flour by dipping method or sift. Stir
flour and salt together. Blend in. Mix in nuts.
Chill dough. Heat oven to 350°. Roll dough
into 1" balls. Place on ungreased baking sheet.
Cookies do not spread. Bake 10-12 min. or
until set, but not brown. While still warm, roll
in confectioners' sugar. Cool and roll in sugar
again. Makes 4 doz.

Chocolate Drops

2 T. butter
1 can sweetened condensed milk (15 oz.)
1 C. flour
1 t. vanilla
9 oz. chocolate chips
1 C. chopped nuts

Melt butter and chocolate over boiling water. When melted remove from stove and stir in milk. Add flour and mix well. Finally, add nuts and vanilla. Drop by teaspoonfuls on well greased baking sheet about 2 in. apart. Bake 10 min. at 325°. Remove from pan while hot. Makes 3 doz. cookies that taste like fudge candy or 5 doz. small cookies.

GINGER SNAPS

3/4 C. shortening
3/4 C. butter
2 3/4 C. sugar (divided)
2 eggs
2 t. baking soda
2 t. cinnamon
2 t. cloves
2 t. ginger
1/2 C. molasses
4 C. flour

Cream shortening. Work in 2 C. sugar.
Mix until light. Beat in eggs and molasses
thoroughly. Sift dry ingredients together and
gradually mix with creamy batter. Beat well.
Dough may be soft. Chill. Roll into 1" balls
and roll in remaining sugar. Place on greased
baking sheet. Bake at 350° for 12-15 min. Let
stand 1 min. Remove from pan and cool on
wire rack. Makes 100 cookies.

ALMOND BARK COOKIES

2 lbs. almond bark
  2 C. Rice Krispies
  2 C. Captain Crunch Peanut butter cereal
  2 C. miniature marshmallows (colored)
  1 C. Spanish peanuts

Melt almond bark in 200° oven. When warm turn off oven and stir until soft. Mix in remaining ingredients and drop on wax paper. Cool.

SPRITZ

    1 C. butter
  1/2 C. sugar
      1 egg
  1/2 t. almond extract
2 1/2 C. flour
      food coloring (optional)

Cream butter. Add sugar and beat until fluffy. Beat in egg and almond extract. Blend in flour. Add food coloring. Fill cookie press. Form into desired shapes and decorate. Bake at 350° for 8-10 min.

PEANUT BUTTER BLOSSOMS

    1 C. margarine
    1 C. sugar
        2 eggs
    1 C. peanut butter
    1 C. packed brown sugar
    1 t. vanilla

2 1/2 C. flour
    1 t. baking soda
    1 t. baking powder
    1 t. salt

        chocolate kisses

Mix first 6 ingredients until fluffy. Add next 4 ingredients and mix well. Shape into 1" balls and roll in sugar. Place 2" apart on ungreased cookie sheet. Bake at 350° for 12-15 min. Press chocolate kiss on cookie. May be chilled before baking to make it easier to handle.

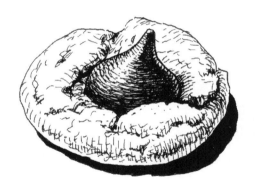

RICE KRISPY BALLS

1 C. white sugar
1 C. white corn syrup
1 C. peanut butter
6 C. Rice Krispies

Heat sugar and corn syrup until boiling. Remove from heat and add the peanut butter and Rice Krispies. Make into small balls and cool. You can coat the balls with melted almond bark (add a little oil to the almond bark).

Chocolate Snow Balls

3/4 C. brown sugar
1 t. vanilla
1 egg
2 C. flour
1 t. baking powder
1/4 t. baking soda
3/4 C. butter or margarine
1/4 C. milk
3 oz. unsweetened chocolate (melted)
1 C. walnuts (chopped fine)
1/2 t. salt

Mix sugar and butter well. Add vanilla, chocolate, egg, and then the remaining ingredients. Chill until you can make into balls the size of walnuts. Place on ungreased cookie sheet 2" apart. Bake at 350° for 8-10 min. Remove from cookie sheet carefully while hot. Roll in powdered sugar. Cool. Redo in powdered sugar.

BRILLIANT SLICES

      1 C. butter
        1 egg
2 1/2 C. flour
      1 C. confectioners' sugar
      1 t. vanilla
      1 C. pecans or walnuts (chopped)
      1 C. green candied cherries (sliced)
      1 C. red candied cherries (sliced)

Cream butter and sugar. Blend egg and vanilla with flour. Stir nuts and cherries into mixture. Shape long rolls. Chill 3 hrs. Cut in slices. Place on ungreased cookie sheet. Bake at 350° for 12-15 min.

Snowflakes

        1/2 C. sugar
        1/3 C. butter or margarine
            1 egg
        1/2 t. vanilla
    1 1/4 C. flour
        1/2 t. baking powder
        1/2 t. salt
    6 oz. pkg. semi-sweet chocolate chips (melted)
            chopped nuts

Mix well sugar, butter, egg, and vanilla.
Sift dry ingredients together and blend into
shortening mixture. Chill 1 hr. Heat oven to
375°. Roll dough into 1/8" thick on floured
board. Cut into small stars. Bake on ungreased
baking sheet 6-8 min. until lightly browned.
Cool. Put two cookies together with melted
sweet chocolate. Add dab of chocolate and
sprinkle chopped nuts on top. Makes 32.

TRILBYS

- 1 C. brown sugar
- 1 C. butter or shortening
- 2 C. oatmeal
- 2 C. flour
- 1/2 C. sour milk
- 1 t. baking soda

Cream sugar and butter. Dissolve soda in sour milk. Add other ingredients and mix well. Roll thin. I use a medium size round cutter. Bake at 350° for 10-12 min. until edges brown.

Filling:

- 1 lb. pitted dates
- 1/2 C. water
- 1 C. sugar

Boil until thick and smooth. Put filling between two cookies.

LEMON SNOWDROPS

    1 C. butter or margarine
1/2 C. confectioners' sugar
    2 C. flour
  1/4 t. salt
    1 t. lemon extract

Heat oven to moderate heat (375°). Cream butter and sugar. Add lemon extract, flour, and salt. Mix well. Measure level t. of dough. Round into balls and flatten slightly. Place 1" apart on ungreased baking sheet. Bake 8-10 min. until lightly browned. Cool.

Lemon butter filling:
Blend 1 egg, slightly beaten, grated rind of 1 lemon, 2/3 C. sugar, 3 T. lemon juice and 1 1/2 T. softened butter in top of double boiler. Cook over hot water until thick, stirring constantly. Set aside to cool and put between two cookies. Roll in confectioners' sugar.

GUM DROP JEWELS

    1 C. butter
    1 C. packed brown sugar
      1 egg
    1 t. vanilla
1 3/4 C. flour
   1/2 t. baking soda
   1/2 t. baking powder
   1/2 t. salt
    1 C. quick oatmeal
    1 C. cut up gum drops (no black drops)
   1/2 C. chopped nuts

In bowl cream butter. Gradually add sugar and beat until light and fluffy. Beat in eggs and vanilla. Stir together flour, soda, baking powder, and salt. Gradually add to creamed mixture. Stir in rolled oats, gum drops, and nuts. Drop by rounded t. onto greased cookie sheet. Bake at 350° for 12-14 min. Cool on wire rack. Makes 5-6 doz.

THUMBPRINT COOKIES

1/2 C. shortening (part butter)
1/4 C. brown sugar
   1 egg separated
 1/2 t. vanilla
  1 C. flour
 1/4 t. salt
3/4 C. finely chopped nuts
     jelly, candied cherries, or tinted
     confectioners' sugar icing

Heat oven to 350°. Mix shortening, sugar, egg yolk, and vanilla thoroughly. Blend together flour and salt. Stir in. Roll into balls (1 t.) Beat egg white slightly with fork. Dip balls in egg white and roll in nuts. Place 1" apart on ungreased baking sheet. Press thumbs gently in center of each. Bake 10-12 min. or until set. Cool. Fill thumb prints with jelly, candied cherries, or tinted icing. Makes 3 doz.

TINGALINGS

1 pkg. chocolate chips (12 oz.)
 1/2 t. salt
1/2 C. raisins
 1 C. chopped nuts
1/2 C. chopped dates
 3 C. corn flakes
1/2 C. coconut

Melt chocolate over hot water. Add remaining
ingredients to chocolate. Drop by t. onto
wax paper. Set in cool place until chocolate
hardens.

JAN HAGEL

- 1 C. butter or margarine
- 1 C. sugar
- 1 egg (separated)
- 2 C. flour
- 1/2 t. cinnamon
- 1 T. water
- 1/2 C. finely chopped walnuts

Heat oven to 350°. Lightly grease a jelly roll pan (15 1/2"x10 1/2"x1"). Mix butter, sugar, and egg yolk. Blend flour and cinnamon. Stir into butter mixture. Pat into pan. Beat water and egg white until frothy. Brush over dough. Sprinkle with nuts. Bake 20-25 min. or until done (lightly brown). Cut immediately into squares.

MINT SURPRISE

   3 C. flour
   1 t. baking soda
 1/2 t. salt
   1 C. butter (half shortening may be used)
   1 C. sugar
 1/2 C. firmly packed brown sugar
    2 eggs
   2 T. water
   1 t. vanilla
1 pkg. chocolate mint candy wafers
      colored sugar or walnut halves

Sift together flour, soda, and salt. Cream butter, gradually adding sugar and brown sugar. Blend in eggs, water, and vanilla. Beat well. Add dry ingredients. Mix thoroughly. Cover and refrigerate at least 2 hours. Enclose each wafer in about 1 T. chilled dough. Place on baking sheet 2" apart. You may top with colored sugar or a walnut half. Bake at 350° for 10-12 min. Makes 4 1/2 doz.